Multicultural Mindfulness

Other books by Nora D'Ecclesis…

Mastering Tranquility: Developing Powerful Stress Management Skills

Tranquil Seas: Applying Guided Visualization

Reiki Roundtable

The Retro Budget Prescription: Skillful Personal Planning

I'm So Busy! Efficient Time Management

Lock Your Door: Passwords, PINS & Hackers

Haiku: Natures Meditation

Adult Coloring: Be a Kid Again!

Equanimity & Gratitude

Tick-Borne: Questing to Vampire

Twin Flame: A Novella

Spiritual Portals: A Historical Perspective

MULTICULTURAL MINDFULNESS

NOURISHING THE SOUL

BY NORA D'ECCLESIS

Published by Renaissance Presentations, LLC
King of Prussia, PA
ISBN 978-1-7330201-1-4
1st Edition: June, 2020

Dedication

Colonel Diana Brown

This book is dedicated to an amazingly compassionate woman who serves as a commander in the USAF. Our paths crossed a decade ago and my life has never been the same. We are kindred spirits and wonderful best friends. Diana is a born leader who balances her mission in the Air Force with her mindful approach to staying in the present. She is a friend who is always available, supportive and motivates me to kick it up a notch.

"Yes Ma'am!"

Multicultural Mindfulness During COVID-19

My mindfulness practice has served me well for almost three decades. I was reflecting last night on the benefits as I complete my new book on mindfulness. It seems I have been training as a mindful meditator my entire life for a lifestyle that includes so many techniques for quality and quantity of life but three stand out during these days of the 2020 pandemic virus:

- The use of the NAMASTE greeting at ten feet without touching but sending energetic love and compassion is the best way to greet people.

- During zazen we let the itch on our nose to come and go without scratching it or touching our faces.

- Mindfulness style includes intense cleanliness and single tasking clean-up.

Multicultural Mindfulness: Nourishing the Soul

The non-judgmental acceptance of the feelings that emerge in our thoughts and emotions, in the present, manifests into a lifelong mindful practice. Mindfulness is cultivated from an intention to viewing things as they manifest in the moment to moment, not the past or the future. It is the interoceptive awareness that acts as the catalyst to dig deep inside our body to allow this transformation. Mindfulness is a state of conscious awareness of surroundings, unencumbered by judgmental attitudes and thoughts which tend to restrict the ability to place into context the attitudes and feelings in relation to the world as we find it, rather than the world we imagined we are in.

Mindfulness vitiates the tendency to add or subtract inappropriate feelings or attitudes in our perceptions of the world surrounding us, helps us see the world as it is and guides us away from inadequate or false interpretations of the world we wish we were in. Most importantly, mindfulness helps us remain in the present rather than expending effort dealing with the unknowable future or unresolved issues of the past.

The similarities of the various modalities found around the world to practice mindfulness are more numerous than the differences in some cases than the activities of a culture. They are passed down from generation to generation with the name of the activity rather than the more trending term of mindfulness. Make no mistake the names change from countries and cultures around the globe, but the intention is identical. Join me on a journey of how mindfulness exists in other cultures with the diversity and of the way things are done in other countries to formulate a lifestyle of staying in the present.

There is no doubt that many of us experience stress throughout the day in both our personal and professional lives. Sometimes we do not even realize how tense we are until we set aside a moment to sit down and take a personal inventory of how we are feeling. Do you have a mind racing with thoughts and constant lists of tasks that need to be accomplished? Do you notice areas of your body that are constantly tense? Are you living in a perpetual state of stress? Stress can have a variety of harmful effects on the body and mind from depression, anxiety, sleep disorders, headaches and ulcers.

It is well documented that stress has a profound impact on the health of the body and mind.

As an example, let's take a look at the number one killer in the United States for both men and women: heart disease. Numerous research studies suggest that the following psychological factors have an impact on the development and progression of heart disease: depression, anxiety, anger and stress. A study indicated that people with depression are more than two times as likely to experience a cardiac event, such as heart attack, surgery or death, than a non-depressed individual. One way to turn the tides of this terrible disease process, and all others related to fight or flight stress is to prevent it before irreversible damage is done. It is time to claim back our lives and bring ourselves into harmony with a natural state of healing and well-being that can be accessed by anyone as a result of mindful living. A mind and body that is constantly bombarded with stress signals a stimulation of the sympathetic nervous system which never has time to recover. Eventually, it is as if we become carried away by the momentum of stress, and we forget how to be any other way.

Taking time throughout the day to go into an opposite state of relaxation, rest, calm and happiness reminds our body that there is more than one way to be. The goal is to turn the momentum in the other direction. Let's attempt to make calm our baseline, the norm to which our body always returns.

Challenging situations will always arise and stress in certain situations can be a healthy way to keep us focused on handling a problem or accomplishing a task. However, once the challenge is over, many bodies fail to return to a restful state because we are so accustomed to stress and anxiety. In order to accomplish this baseline of tranquility, we must immerse ourselves in activities that bring about this state of rest.

One technique that has proven to be especially effective in the area of stress reduction is the mindfulness of guided visualizations.

A mindfulness practice is a way to bring our lives back into balance and mitigate the effects of stress on the minds, bodies and spirits of those who practice. Some forms of meditation instruct practitioners to bring single pointed focus to their breath or to a mantra, a short phrase that is repeated over and over. It can be difficult to sustain this type of practice because our minds have become accustomed to racing with a variety of thoughts, and our bodies are programed for productivity. While mindfulness and mantra meditation, if practiced consistently throughout one's life, can certainly bring about calm and insight, many end up abandoning the practice before they are able to realize any of the potential benefits. This could be the result of time management, self-discipline or expense of mindfulness programs.

The purpose of mantras is to keep the mind focused and to perhaps guide the practitioner towards transcendental states through forgetting oneself and breaking past the boundaries of the ego-mind. Why does a mantra necessarily have to be one phrase? Could a mantra not be an entire guided visualization meditation? This would serve a similar purpose.

Guided visualizations bring the mind into single pointed concentration, allowing distractions of a racing mind to drop away. In fact, guided visualizations can be even more effective in achieving this end because it engages the mind, body and spirit in an all-inclusive journey. Guided imagery calls all of the senses together by leading one into a scenario where sight, sound, smell, touch, action, feeling and emotion are activated. Engaging the entire body enhances the ability to sustain a concentrated state. We begin our global journey of how various cultures and countries practice mindfulness with a visual from my childhood: climbing the magnolia tree on my grandfather's property.

By March the snow is dirty on the sides of the road and the piles of ice in the shopping mall lots simply nasty to navigate. On Groundhogs Day, Punxsutawney Phil predicted six more weeks of winter. The warmth of the spring sun will soon appear with longer days and the end of icy roads. The spring equinox brings with it the rebirth we crave when things simply begin to become oppressive. With each March the weather comes in like a lion still hovering between winter and summer. The winds are cold and the rain icy and damp and just when we can't stand it the morning sun burns bright and the warmth is powerful. The skies turn blue with clear weather clouds and it is on that day we know the spring is almost here. Winter ends in the eastern United States as quickly as it begins.

Open the door to the great outdoors and feel the warmth of the first spring breeze. Enter the yard to explore the joys of nature during the transitional season of rebirth. The fragrant scents of the season pound the sense of smell. The honeysuckle is over-powering walking near the long line of shrubs with beautiful white flowers hanging waiting to be picked and tasted by pulling the pistil and its nectar from each flower.

The magnificence of the magnolia trees and the pink flowers entice us to climb up into the arms of the branches as we did as kids, innocent and loving the gentle scent from the flowing petals.

The buds from the dogwood will blossom into the pinks and whites of cross like structures. Small but mighty trees with the spiritual wonders of hope.

Walking slowly across the yard we see the buds on the huge oaks are ready to burst open with the promise of a new day, a new season, another chance.

Popping out of the ground still cold from the winter ice is the crocus, first out and proud of it. The crocus is followed by the pansies, daffodils and impatiens. Warm rains help to encourage the spring growth.

Everything about this warmth of the spring season prepares us for the joys of planting, weeding and watering. Encourage it. The herbs come first with careful preparation of the pots. Parsley will stand up to the cool nights, so it is planted first, then the mints as we almost taste them in our teas and meats. Finally, the basil, which needs more sun and warm summer nights, or it will not survive. Tending to the wildflowers and roses and rhododendron shrubs balances out the gardening, some fruits… some vegetables… some herbs. Variety is the spice of gardening and the garden comes alive in the spring.

Pruning the roses, digging a plot for tomatoes and eggplant, trimming the azaleas we are outside in the fresh air enjoying the nurturing rays of the sun. Mowing the lawn and smelling the fresh cut grass, walking back and forth making beautiful lines as we follow the mower is meditative and mindful, as valuable as a walking meditation. Up and down back and forth forgetting the mental chatter, the problems at the office, the decisions that need to be made, just being here and now in the present. Walking thru the gardens preparing and seeding is in the now. Notice the blue jays chattering, the cardinals and scarlet tanagers brighten up the vibrant colors of nature and the little chipmunks making chirpy sounds as they run and scamper about preparing for the new life of this spring.

FRILUFSLIV (free-loofts-liv)

Norway

In 1859 the word friluftsliv (free-loofts-liv) was coined in Norway to express the cultural joy of being outdoors and breathing the air while in nature. Norwegian playwright Henrik Ibsen using the term friluftsliv created a character who 'needs' to be alone and in nature. The word frilufsliv had been used in Norway by other artists but Ibsen made it a colloquialism.

> Paa Vidderne "On the Heights" by Henrik Ibsen
> In the lonely seter cottage
> My abundant catch I gather;
> There is hearth, a stool, a table,
> Frilufsliv for my thoughts

Half the world lives in urban areas with limited access to mountains and lakes and nature. In Norway getting out into nature is the national mindfulness of free - air - life philosophy to the mountains, fjords, glaciers and coastlines. Ice fishing is a sport practiced by many and readily available to a nation of people who love the great outdoors in both summer and winter.

The freedom to roam is codified in Norwegian laws. Allemnsretten 'everyman's rights' is a concept that enables hikers on their respective mindfulness walks to enjoy the uncultivated land owned by others. They can hike the countryside without the owner's permission and even camp there for a night 150 meters away from buildings. These nature hikes are done by many either alone or in small groups as a way of clearing their minds of past problems or the worrisome future. The only caution is to find a clear area if camping the night or the holly bow which covers so much of the landscape might ruin the moment with present scratchy underbrush. Norway brings new meaning to outdoorsy mindfulness awareness and there are so many participating that information on the positive effects such as improved thinking skills and reduction of ADHD even in adults, are being documented.

The ice fishing in Norway is an amazingly mindful experience. The day breaks with a bright clear blue sky. It's the kind of day that beckons one to rise early in order to enjoy the serenity of the clear blue lake before the fish begin feeding and bringing the area just beneath the ice to a frenzy of activity known only to the ice fisher. This is the time when the fisherman/woman know that catches come quickly and numerous as the fish participate in anything that they can find to eat beneath the frozen lake. It is an exciting time to be out on the frozen lake. Walking out on the ice and cutting a hole is a ritual involving the precision of any sport that requires mindfulness.

Ice fishing in Norway is a time of relaxation and contemplation. The fish appear indiscriminate in what they swim to feed on and usually take the bait. All fish caught are consumed.

Nothing is quite so calming as dropping a line and slowly retracting the baited hook while anticipating the tug of the fish when it takes the bait, the essence of fishing, and bringing home a meal. A practice, a skill staying in the present.

Snowing Like a Russian Novel:
Perfect Day for a Meditative Nordic Ski Adventure

It's snowing like a Russian novel with freezing temperatures, but you move forward because today is the day you will Nordic ski. Feel the wind and ice forming on your face and every area of exposed skin. Walk slowly toward the paths available in the clearing. North will take you down a trail of prepared pites or parallel groves cut in the snow. It is neatly cut by machines and frequently the choice of the cross-country skier. South heads out into a mountain of snow untouched by anything except nature. The choice is obvious. With the full realization that opening a track through deep snow can be arduous you move forward, placing your snow boots into the ski and picking up your poles. The basket at the end of each pole assures you that you won't sink too deeply into the beautiful white powder. The poles pushing off of the classic ski motion, left leg push right pole, right leg push left pole. Rhythmic, repetitive motion gliding with each stride releasing endorphins and keeping you in the now. The poles for steadiness and propulsion feel like extensions of your arms and move with you as extended limbs.

Rhythmic, pulsating, gliding forward on flat terrain up and down small hills without breaking the stride of this walking meditation. Left, right, left, right there is no thinking now only the beautiful cadence of the rhythm. If you are thinking you are not meditating.

Feel the pulse of the motion and the joy of being out in the natural beauty of the winter forest. See your breath as you exhale in the cold crisp air and feel the rhythm of your breathing in sync with the movement of the skis. You are alone and at peace with your solitude. The isolation and lack of communication is growing on you as you leave the sounds of the city behind. They are exchanged with sounds of winter birds chirping, little red foxes looking out from behind their hutches and magnificent bucks with brown shaggy fur snorting like ponies. The smells of the forest are overwhelming with the heightened senses in this environment. All of the cabins have cedar aroma from burning logs in their fireplaces. Breathe in the beauty and breathe out the stressors. There is a familiar smell of family and fun and a spiritual awakening from the pine forest, bringing up memories of joyful Christmas aromas. Breathe in the joyful scents and breathe out the mental disquietude. Stop for a rest and sip nourishment from your water bottle.

Replenish your cells with the fluid of life. Value the moment and allow yourself to be happy. Relish the moment as feeling really alive with gratitude for who you are and what you have. Prepare to climb the hill in front of you as there will always be hills and valleys in life. Spreading your skis out so they look like the letter V, herringbone up the hill with a passion to reach the other side, feeling a sense of accomplishment as your reach the crest.

Take a deep breath and push off to glide down the hill at a faster speed pointing your skis inward to snowplow and control your descent. Acceptance that change is inevitable for the rest of this ride because at the bottom is a frozen lake. Hitting the lake at full speed in the skating motion of the cross-country skier allows you to change on a dime as is often the case with the trials and tribulations of life. Pushing first with the right leg as an ice skater and shifting all of your weight to the right leg you find your cadence once again and soon settle in with a feeling of balance and grace gliding through life and across the large lake to the other side. Transfer your weight to control the glide and slide into the snow completing the journey with a feeling of success, a joyful job well-done and the serenity of the meditation known as mastering tranquility.

GEMUTLICHKEIT (guh-myoot-lik-kyt)

Germany

In Germany gemutlichkeit is a mindful concept revolving around social acceptance. It promotes a sense of belonging and feelings of cheer and friendship. In the United States city of Jefferson, Wisconsin has the motto of "The Gemutlichkeit City" promising a cozy sense of joy and warmth while visiting. This has been brought over to American by German Americans who love the social acceptance from their homeland. Gemutlichkeit provides a memorable experience that traditionally includes a variety of beers, barrel polka dancing and of course the culinary delight of cheese curds. The goal is a joyful feeling of food, drink and feeling a part of a celebration. The socialization process guarantees an instant camaraderie of friendly like-minded people. The key is staying in the present for that snapshot of time there is no past, no future just the joy of getting and staying in the moment.

The relaxation of Gemutlichkeit is in the present moment and somewhat unique to German culture. The Germans leave their problems at the door and enter a social environment where everyone is a friend and is made to feel they do in fact "belong"

It is a large gathering and social process not usually found with just a few people in a home, but in a large public venue with the intention set to simply relax. The recharging that occurs is mindful and allows pointless activity to simply relax and have fun. It's a time for people to enjoy social acceptance while staying in the present moment. They are in fact learning to be content. They will emerge more likely to be content with what they have rather than experiencing the torment of what they don't have.

Majestic View of the Snow-Capped Bavarian Alps

Prepare for a meditative journey high above the Alps where the lenticular clouds hover like a massive dome over the range. Calm your body and refocus your mind lie face up with your hands and legs relaxed and your head and neck on a pillow. Focus on your breath, only the breath let thoughts go. Inhale, exhale... inhale, exhale, inhale, exhale, inhale and hold it.

5, 4, 3, 2, 1.

Now exhale.

Your body is releasing tension. Feel your jaw relax and your shoulders sink down into the mat, your legs feel as if you are floating. Inhale cool air and fill your body. Exhale the tense hot air you have been holding. Your body is totally relaxed. Replace negative thoughts with positive affirmations. Set your intention to climb up and out of your stressful existence. Visualize yourself floating on a soft white cumulous cloud. It is cotton like and puffy and looks like cauliflower. It is the fair-weather cloud and a nice place to be. Living our lives in calmness and fair weather. Visualizing the serenity of equanimity and loving kindness. Hold on to your cloud and be safe, protected from all the ups and downs that the pressures of life toss at us. Hold on and experience the tranquility of your ride as a place you want to be in this lifetime. You are rising up now as your cloud moves higher relaxed and resting with your arms and legs stretched out and floating. Look at the panoramic view of the mountain range. Looking up to see the nimbus and cirrus clouds. The gray covering that appears to be curling locks of hair almost in ringlets is misting with a slight drizzle. As in life when we are faced with the fog we hold tight to our fair-weather cloud and move forward. Now in view the rain, snow sleet and hail from a dark nimbus high about the horizon but it passes quickly if we maintain the evenness of equanimity. We visualize ourselves holding our place on the fair-weather cloud and break through the storms to the majestic view of the snow-capped mountain range. Open your heart and eyes to natures beauty.

Enjoy the ride with gratitude for the ability to see and feel and smell the wondrous sights of a magnificent mountain range. Gratitude for what we do have. Gratitude for our good health and love of family and friends.

Ride down now on your tranquil cloud to the bottom of the mountain to a calming visual of resting near a beautiful stream that is filled by the snow running off the mountain. Feel the safety of the ground beneath you and knowing you are firmly grounded to earth's magnetic core. Grounded, in survival skills that serve you in life in the day to day trials and tribulations. Grounded in your ability to maintain balance in the face of any adversity. Begin to slowly stretch as you sit up to take a last look at the serene stream flowing gently past your feet.

Move your fingers and wiggle your toes. Open your eyes and breathe deeply. From the seated position rise slowly and stand tall. Raise your hands up toward the mountain toward the sky and say: "I am grateful for my good health and love of family and friends."

KEYIF

Turkey

Watching the rhythmic flow of the rushing Bosporus is a calming idle pleasure. The majestic Bosporus is an inner strait connecting the Black Sea and the sea of Marmara. It separates the city. On one side it is the European continent and the other Asian forming a natural continental boundary. The word is Bosporus is taken to mean the cow passage after the Greek Mythology of Hera catching Zeus cheating yet again and ultimately the other woman being turned into a cow. It was the seat of the Roman Empire for a thousand years and called Constantinople. After that the Ottoman Empire established a thriving city of Islamic culture.

It is said "that a single cup of coffee has a memory of forty years." In Istanbul the mindfulness of making and drinking Turkish coffee exemplify the serenity and well-being of staying in the present.

Keyif is an Arabic term translating for the most part to 'contentment'. Strolling along the Bosporus in Istanbul the cultural joy Keyif manifests into a mindful practice. The stroll is exactly that, a mindful leisurely walk alone or with a small group enjoying the beauty of the scenic body of water and then stopping to gossip or talk about controversial topics such as politics, religion or finance. One obligatory stop would be at the Mangal barbeque outdoor grill to enjoy the sensory stimulation of the wet tobacco leaves. The open pit barbecues produce delicious chicken, lamb and fish meals. The plan to eat fish and soujuk sausage is joyfully the plan in the present. The goal is to simply walk out and avoid anything that resembles their daily lives. It is a very personal moment of relaxation sitting along the back or from Yali houses build on the waterway. The views are magnificent of people swimming, fishing, traveling over the suspension bridges between continents or taking the ferries.

The Keyif Mindfulness practice is simply taking a walk with no destination, talking about fun stuff if socialization occurs, or just sitting on a bench watching life as it exists in the moment. The practice of preparing Turkish coffee exemplifies the ritual that takes our mind from the disquietude of daily stress to the joy of the present moment. Anticipating the strong aroma and delicious taste of the Turkish cup of coffee. The coffee maker prepares by placing the needed implements needed to prepare the perfect cup of coffee on the counter. Coffee beans are placed in the grinder and ground to an ultra-fine texture almost to a powder like flour. The copper pot to boil water is filled with three cup of room temperature water. Three teaspoons of sugar are dropped in but not stirred to facilitate the caramelization effect.

As the water simmers at low heat the three heaping teaspoons of the powdered coffee is placed in the pot. A visual foam appears within minutes and a teaspoon of that extraordinary foam is placed in each serving cup. One final minute back on the heat assures the coffee maker that more foam will form before the coffee is poured into each serving cup. It is Turkish tradition to drink water to clear the palate before enjoying the deep rich taste of the Turkish coffee enjoyed by all in Istanbul and around the world. Staying in the present moment while making it and then the incredible taste bud sensation of one component of KEYIF!

Down The Shore

The sound of the waves crashing against the jetty precedes the sight of the sea. Walking through the dunes, you can hear and smell the ocean before your feet touch the sand and you place your chair in the perfect position. Open the chair and drop your towel. Spread the beach blanket down on the warm white sand. On this day it seems as white as salt. As you sit and get comfortable look up at the gorgeous white cumulus clouds in the perfectly powder blue sky. They are fluffy like cotton and inform us the sun will shine all day.

The sun's rays permeate the organs of your body and hit every inch of exposed skin. Feel the warmth. Feel the power of the Vitamin D you absorb and its healing energy.

The waves continue to crash creating white caps as high as the boardwalk. The pounding of those waves creates both an excitement and anticipation of becoming one with the sea. Reach for your boogie board now and get up from your chair and start walking toward the sea. Walk faster and then a little faster. Now run at top speed the way you did as a small child knowing you were safe and loved by the family and friends who took you to the beach. Run into the sea kicking past the small white caps and jumping them crashing into the waves head on. Place your body on the board in preparation for the ride in. Turn your head just enough to see the perfect curl of the wave that will carry you all the way into shore.

You feel as if you are floating now as you ride the surf with not a care in the world. No past. No future. Just right now in the present and the closest you will come to levitating. Standing up after that wonderful ride pick up the board and charge back in repeating that first with the boogie board and then getting adventuresome and body surfing in many more waves until your body feels fully alive with a tranquility that you set as your intention. Walk softly back to your beach towel and place your body flat down with your eyes closed and resting in a yoga-like Savassana. Think of nothing, just feel. Feel the joy of knowing you are safe and loved and happy in your choices. Feel the sun again to work its miracle, natures healing rays. Smell the fish and ocean scents. Taste the salt on your lips. Listen to the sounds of the waves moving in and out with the flow of the tides and believe that this is the moment you need to take with you back into the world where we live our lives. Knowing that you have the power to master tranquility as you walk back to your Yali.

"Take your seat on the shore. Listen to the ancient voice in the waves. Taste the salt of life on your tongue. Run your fingers through the eternal sand. Breathe deeply. If you find yourself worrying about your cell phone and emails, if you find yourself feeling guilty that you should be doing "something important," breathe deeply again. And again. Breathe deeply until every fabric of your being is reminded that this, being here, is your top priority. This is peace. This is wisdom. The work is a means to living, but this is the living." - Brian Vaszily

Il Lungo Tavolo

Italy

Il Lungo Tavolo or the Long Table is the epitome of mindfully enjoying the social interaction and preparation of the great meals Italians are known for both in Italy and in Italian American homes in the USA. They maintain the focus on the present while savoring the aromas and preparation of the culture. The weekend time with family and friends includes this five-course sustenance for spiritual as well as good health.

The mindfulness of the Italian cook begins in the market as he or she hand selects the perfectly ripe tomatoes, romaine lettuce, cheeses and antipasto meats. The food is sampled from the fresh cuts of a genuine butcher and sniffed for freshness. Using all sense available to a sentient being the tomato is first seen then touched and finally there is the sniff test! The plum tomatoes selected must be the correct size and color and texture to make the perfect sauce/gravy. All ingredients are written on the "the list" as a metacognitive technique so the meal prep is extraordinary. Ironically the exact amounts of ingredients are never written. The lessons learned in this ancient ritual are handed down verbally from generation to generation and even than a pinch normally replaces the more formal tsp. calibration in most recipes.

Preparation is a sacred art carefully orchestrated and ritualized. Pots, pans and sharp knives are placed near the appropriate counters or range in the kitchen and cooking begins.

The meal starts with a Campari. The Antipasto is the staple starter which traditionally includes olives, pepperoncini, anchovies, artichoke hearts, soppressata or cured dried sausage with just a hint of red pepper, prosciutto, Genoa salami, capicola, pancetta and bruschetta. The "salumi" are cured salted meats mostly made from pork.

The second course is lasagna which is a wide flat noodle baked in layers interspersed with ricotta cheese and parsley and chopped beef with a minimum of ragu.

The third course, cooked vegetables. A favorite of broccoli rabe is served steaming hot. Broccoli rabe is actually not broccoli but from the turnip family. It's a milder tasting with dark green leaves and a little bitter.

The fourth course is Fiorentina steak, a large T-bone steak from the loin of Chianina cows farms in Tuscany. Each side of the steak is cooked for five minutes and served rare.

The fifth course includes cannoli the pastry from Sicily stuffed with a creamy ricotta cheese and put into a tube deep fried pastry crust. Tiramisu is a coffee cake made with sponge fingers and cocoa powder, espresso and limoncello poured over ice getting its flavor from the lemon peel so not sour as an after-dinner liquor.

Sentiero Azzurro

Built on terraces for growing grapes and olives that overlook the Mediterranean Sea, the Cinque Terre provides an exquisitely mindful hike thru connected towns colloquially called the "five lands."

We walk the path mindfully and in the present without judgement or interaction.

The relationship between people and environment in mindful procession, as we ascend thru the villages as the path becomes precarious with less stable footing, symbolic of the joys and sorrows in life. The paths wind upward from what was once the republic of Genoa built as forts and defense towers to fend off repeated invasions.

We walk the path mindfully and in the present without judgement or interaction.

Cinque Terre is now a national park under UNESCO so as we walk from Monterosso al Mare to Venazza then Monarola to Rio Maggiore and finally the top and Corniglia, we must stop and show our tickets, smiling and proceeding upward staying in the present.

We walk the path mindfully and in the present without judgement or interaction.

The fragrant wildflowers along the paths bring a pleasant feeling of peacefulness and gratitude. The tall building built on the side of the cliff are pastel in color and calming. With the realization that walking thru the tunnels is also a part of history from the 11th Century we walk silently and with the mindset of spiritual journey.

We walk the path mindfully and in the present without judgement or interaction.

At the top, the view is magnificent, we end the journey with homemade gelato, pears grown on the cliffs and of course authentic Italian pasta. We make a final stop at the Church of San Pietro in the village and give thanks.

We walk the path mindfully and in the present without judgement or interaction.

SHIRIN-YOKU

Japan

Japan is a smorgasbord of mindfulness practices. Forest bathing, Tea Ceremony and Zazen meditation have been selected to represent this diverse culture.

Shinrin-Yoku: Forest bathing has a had huge following since the 1980's focusing on the sounds of birds and the wind in the trees as people walk in small groups or alone into the natural environment of a forest. It is mindful experience slowing down the person and staying in the present. Close attention and awareness focus on the environs, seeing insects watching the squirrels and hiking in a contemplative format.

It is sometimes a small group with leadership looking for items in the forest to mindfully train the eye to be more observant. The process is clear direction but maintains the mindful purpose. Careful collection of items to be observed and savored is encouraged. It includes occasionally a walk to a secluded area to remove any unnecessary clothing for the adventure. Always present is the intention of what needs to be washed away. An amazing roundtable discussion after the forest bathing might include laughing, crying, sharing and healing with others learning about their stories. This results in the completely conscious effort and subsequent healing of the experience. Forest bathing in Japan is a walk in the mountains under the trees... "taking in the forest."

The Japanese Tea Ceremony is called Chado and means the Way of Tea. It is the ceremonial preparation and serenity of the traditions that inform us Chado is the ceremonial quintessential spiritual experience to be repeated exactly in form and as frequently as possible to insure it takes its place as a portal to our mindfulness practice.

The tea ceremony expresses the simplicity of Zen and was initiated by Sen no Riyu in the early 1500's. He brought a simple totally austere method of spiritual mindfulness to the sharing of a cup of tea. Chado is held in a tearoom usually in the center of a fragrant and beautiful natural garden. The entrance to the tearoom includes the Shinto practice of washing hands and mouth to purify before entering. After walking into the tearoom thru the Shoji sliding doors one is greeted by the scent of freshly picked flowers and the beauty of their presence. The entrance itself is low level so guests must bend which is a symbol of humility and everyone being equal in the way of tea as in life. The floor is constructed of tatami mats woven straw of about two meters. The tables are low, and the guests sit on a zabutan.

The tea master carries the tea bowl and whisk, scoop, napkin and tea. Tea Master has also placed the fresh water on the fire to boil in advance of the ceremony. The wastewater has a container which holds the ladle and is placed in position. Each step is done according to a rigidly traditional format for the expressed purpose of a ceremonial meditation that includes respect, purity, tranquility, harmony.

The Serenity Walking Meditation

Mindfully walking one hand closed the other covering it in shaku, feeling each step and the precision of each step. Circumambulating as the Buddha thousands of years ago. From the first step when the ball of the big toe hits the ground, we unite the walking meditation with zazen bringing the stillness of sitting in mediation into action. We stay in the present. We are not thinking of anything. We are mindful. Each step is breathing in and breathing out in synergy with a few steps out. We rise from zazen seated meditation by tilting the torso forward upright about ninety degrees then extending the hips and knees we stand on a mid-foot landing. Letting go of everything and controlling the breath we move forward in peace and equanimity. Kinhin our walking meditation is practiced with our eyes at half-mast looking not at the walls of the zendo or the birds in the tress through the window. When we hear a sound, we simply hear it, so the chirping bird does not excite us and break the walking meditation nor does the fire truck racing down the street with sirens blaring. We do not look up or take note to tell the other meditators how lovely the sound of the bird. We allow the concept of bird chirping then proceed in kinhin.

While walking indoors we might be tempted to cut corners, but this is not best as Zens do not cut corners in the walking meditation or in life. Walking now one foot extending in front of the other, mindfully walking as we meditate with others in a community of spirituality. Today is the day we will exit the solitude of the meditation hall as we walk single file out the door and move toward an outdoor walking meditation. Visualize a huge labyrinth similar to the one in Notre Dame de Chartres in Paris. Our labyrinth sits at the foot of snow-capped mountain in an area of lush trees and gardens. It might be said that walking into a labyrinth is a metaphor for walking toward your core. It is a spiritual experience. Our labyrinth is unicursal, when you walk in and around the way out is exact same way in. It is not a maze or puzzle to be solved, a labyrinth is a path in and out. As we walk in silent meditation into the labyrinth, we pause at the entrance to center ourselves. We encounter other people on the parallel paths. The journey might seem long one time and very short the next. We might be so intent on getting to the end that we miss the subtle sounds, sights, smells of nature. If we are mindful, we notice the small signs that others have passed this way before us...a footprint, a memento left lovingly behind, a stone dislodged by a wayward boot.

We notice our inclination to make everything perfect again, pick up the stone, erase the footprint. We acknowledge the sacredness of the space, cleansed by many feet silently stepping, spiraling through the small path. We feel the connection to all who have traveled this path, and especially to those on it together in community mediation.

We return to meditation center with intention set toward our more spiritual core and silence of seated mediation. Satori, or the experience of awakening, is a little closer.

HYGGE (Hew-Guh)

Denmark

To be in the present and enjoy the moment is the intention. Danish Hygge (Hew-Guh) offers a path toward the comfort and joy of staying in the present which is a way of life in Danish culture. Hygge is a serene retreat into enjoying the simplicity of a cozy and warm environment devoid of the autopilot rushing so common in most cultures.

In Copenhagen, where most of the population joyfully ride their bikes to work and social events, there are bike paths everywhere. During the snow days the bikes paths are plowed first! The major commerce is spread out over the many kilometers of the waterfront city to avoid traffic congestion. The harbor is peacefully shared by their neighboring country, Sweden. The Danes think of themselves as the happiest on earth and with reason when one explores how to Hygge. Sixteen hours of darkness a day in the winter and cold temperatures create the perfect environment to come in out of the cold to a warm cozy tradition.

Hygge started in Norway around the 19th Century but strongly caught on in Denmark becoming intrinsically entwined with their cultural goals. It has recently become a popular word in the British and American lexicons.

Taking time throughout the day to go into a state of relaxation, rest, calm and happiness reminds our body that there is more than one way to be. The goal is to turn the momentum in the other direction away from stress. Hygge makes calm our baseline, the norm to which the body should always return. It also pumps up serotonin and norepinephrine. The simplicity of the Hygge activity is what makes it even more wonderful and it doesn't involve any of the usual materialistic purchases of similar practices.

Hygge, in a word, is mindfulness, being in the present...living a life of being open and in a state of equanimity. Hygge is... a safe haven of enjoying the simple things in life with either alone time or socializing. It's a daily experience during all seasons. In the winter it is the time to come in out of the cold, snuggle with your warm puppy in the sherpa blankets and settle in with friends and family to enjoy the well-being of the moment. The shared glass of wine or tea with Viennoiserie pastries and the flickering of the candles in subdued yellow tones set the mood. The additional warming slippers and fireplace heat omits the mental disquietude and allows for the comfortable socialization of respectful conversation.

More than just part of the daily Dane cultural practice Hygge is the Dane identity including socialization, compassion, respect for all other practices and an awareness that taking that bike out in the morning is, in addition to the environmental benefits, a sound practice toward better quality and quantity of human life. Watching a small group of millennials place a blanket down on the park lawn and pull out the Dane beer "pilsner" and cheese for a Hygge while the sun is out is a joy and comforting for the observer. An actual sunny day is rare with less than four hours of sun a day and a great deal of precipitation. Imagine Hygge in Central Park on a sunny day or the Poconos in February. The joy of a cozy and comfortable conversation with people who respect the diversity of opinions and create a safe environment to simply stay in the moment. Hygge is a way of life in Denmark, the sharing of foods and drink and relaxing alone or in small groups. Light a candle, kick off your boots, build a fire in your wood burning stove and visualize our global neighbors in Copenhagen.

Polaris

On a cool clear night looking up at the sky from a lounge chair on the deck, the constellations are dramatically brighter than normal. A feeling of total tranquility emerges with relaxation often found in natures beauty. The Big Dipper and its seven bright stars look painted in the sky. It is said that the ancient Greeks named Big Dipper "Bear."

They saw the same sky I am joyfully visualizing in a different century. The Greeks have tales from their Gods Zeus and Hera about a squabble over the way Zeus was always philandering with other women so his wife Hera propelled her into the sky where she remains to this day in the Heavens. Who can refute Hera's power if one reflects that Ursa Major never sets below the horizon in mid-northern latitudes. Now the Native Americans knew bears did not have long tales like the Big Dipper, so they taught that tail latitudes were three hunters chasing the bear. During the American Civil War history projects a vision of slaves escaping from the sub-human treatment as they followed the North Star to freedom. They told each other of the drinking gourd helping the underground railroad to find their way north. As history begins to subside in the thoughts a more meditative journey begins...

We look for our personal North Star for guidance when we experience the disquietude of chaos in our lives. Our path points in the direction of our Polaris and the spiritual and emotional elements bringing us toward better quality of life. In our youth it was easy we simply looked up to our parents and teachers who always gave us good direction and set us on a good course. As adults it is more complex formulating our life purpose and search for a constant to draw strength. Ultimately our strength comes from within. We are strong. We are capable of leadership. We are capable of accomplishing everything we want out of life. Do not doubt yourself. Your North Star is now your personalized path. Struggle will always precede great accomplishment. Through it all continue to move forward. Your place on earth is one of great importance. Whether we realize it or not we have all touched other people's lives. Taking good care of our mind body and spirit will allow us to live with our lives with abundance and continue to touch others with love and radiate humble appreciation for all the gifts in life. Many of us desire change in our lives but are unsure how to proceed. Begin by affirming concepts that are essential, yet often forgotten or ignored. Relax and refocus. Appreciate what we have instead of dwelling on what we don't. Remember that change is inevitable. Break with old patterns that hold us back from your potential. Prevent negative thoughts and people from controlling our lives. Remain calm through adversity.

The guiding star directs us to toward a more spiritual life filled with compassion, equanimity and love. Envision yourself as you would like to be, and do not give up that as your mission in life.

Native American Mindfulness

United States of America

Native American tribal practices form the basis for the earliest practice of mindfulness in the USA. They taught a spiritual form of communication using a talking piece. "Calling the Circle" is an interactive and egalitarian technique which includes a spiritual exchange developed by Native Americans. It creates a mindful communication skill with an informal structure that eliminates stress and anxiety and is a joyful way to express thoughts. It is similar to hygge in many ways. There is no stress of public speaking, no one has the obligation to speak if they don't want to. They can defer to the person sitting next to them.

The talking stick is sometimes called a "speakers' staff" and probably was simply the pipe passed by many of the tribes. It is an object that promotes mindfulness and a spiritual exchange of ideas and feelings. In tribal council circle, a talking stick is passed around from member to member allowing only the person holding the stick to speak. In many ways it is more a listening stick. This permits all those present at a council meeting to be heard, especially those present in the circle who tend to be introverted. Talking "lean" precludes the people who talk on forever from dominating the discussion. Speaking and listening from the heart are always part of the process and an excellent rule of speaking spontaneously after receiving the stick prevents the group from thinking about their responses while others are talking. The technique therefore has four precepts or structures. Talking lean, talking spontaneously, listening from the heart and speaking from the heart creating a truly spiritual exchange. The talking stick has been used by Native Americans for centuries. It is now used in America by many groups hoping to encourage mindful communication skills, corporations, government bodies, students. The talking Stick allows both space and time for the person holding it to make a point, to have their say, to be heard.

Talking lean, getting to the point, is a major structure. It is important to be both quick and concise, but also attentive and open to the person who is holding the stick. One by one the people in the circle take the stick or pass not wishing to add anything at the time so the stick moves to the person next to them in clockwise order. Sticking in small circle holding the stick, looking at it, staying in the present and simply feel it in our hands omits all other distractions and mental disquietude. Composing the thoughts before talking the person begins to speak slowly, quietly, concisely with the refined words pared down to the bone. The others in the circle are clearly present and perhaps for the first time listening to the words being provided by another person talking.

They are learning not to think of what to say in response or what needs to be added to the topic at hand. This is not always easy, learning to speak, learning to be quiet, learning to listen, to really listen to another's point of view. The intention is set to explore a specific topic. It is imperative to listen to each other, so it is suggested no one formulates what they plan to say while another is speaking. The style is extemporaneous speaking. The time limits are used as guidelines and the process is mindful.

A historical perspective of the 12th Century, the culture of Indigenous people called Haudenosaunee who lived around 1142 CE. The Haudenosaunee people of the longhouse came from six tribes: Seneca, Onondaga, Oneida, Cayuga, Mohawk and Tuscarora. They met in a grand council circle and after lighting their fire exchanged ideas and opinions. The techniques were mindful and a spiritual ritual of the tribes. The Grand Council, where seventy-five percent of the men and the women had to agree, created spiritual communication skills between civilized groups of people facing each other in an open circle with a fire in the middle. During a circle the participants would sometimes sit in silence for hours only to know the answer and ruling of the majority. This level of spirituality exists in higher levels of consciousness. The fire in the middle represents future generations. There is documentation to indicate that during some circles not one word was ever spoken, the spiritual nature of the group predominated.

The term "Calling the Circle" originated with Christina Baldwin in her book of the same name. The use of a talking piece in combination with a circle of group interaction emulates the early tribes. It is frequently mentioned by participants as the most emotionally liberating event. This ancient practice establishes itself in modern day because of the ever-increasing need for mindful communication.

The Pesse Canoe Glides

A canoe glides through the water with a serene calmness... a boat dug from a pine log... like the first boat ever used... it was called the Pesse canoe in 8000BCE... Pesse... a serene word to describe a serene glide... the visual is of the majestic colors of the white and grey birch... floating down a slow-moving steam... with a hand dangling in the water...

The stern paddler is responsible for steering the canoe... the paddle blade is forward alongside and dipped into the water and then drawn back... The splash of the paddle in the water is calming, rhythmic and meditative. The canoe glides through the water past the honey suckle on the shore, under the Spanish moss hanging from the Bald Cypress and Southern live oak, the trees providing shade from the direct sun. Allow your hand to hang down over the side of the boat and feel the cool lake water run through your fingers. Look over the side into the crystal-clear water as the small mouth bass and trout swim around sucking vegetation for nourishment, spitting it out, sucking more in. Feel the tension begin to diminish and the blood pressure drop, and heart rate become regular.

5, 4, 3, 2, 1.

Your body is releasing tension.

Feel your jaw relax and your shoulders sink down, your legs feel as if you are floating. Inhale cool air and fill your body. Exhale the tense hot air you have been holding.

Your body is totally relaxed. Replace negative thoughts with positive affirmations.

Set your intention to climb up and out of your stressful existence.

The Mindful Runner

Running is, without a doubt, one of the most popular forms of exercise in the world. It is now commonplace for marathons in large cities to fill to capacity with over 20,000 participants. Not only is the number of people who participate in marathons increasing, but so is the number of people who finish them. This speaks to the popularity of a pursuit that has as many mental health benefits as physical ones.

Many runners have switched from logging their miles on asphalt to the more scenic experience of nature trails. Some choose to run in pairs or larger groups because they enjoy the camaraderie or competitive motivation. Others choose to run alone to enhance the mental element that can turn a strenuous activity into a very calming one. The perfect connection between mind and body that occurs during what is affectionately called "runner's high" becomes attainable in part due to the isolation -- the majority of things that can interrupt us during seated meditation are, quite literally, left in the home. The road, and preferably, the trail, provides the impetus necessary to focus on the breath, focus on the rhythm of the feet, and become completely immersed in physical activity.

Follow your breath and attempt to synchronize the movement of your body with the inhalation and exhalation of your lungs. Be present in the environment that surrounds you. Both meditation and running require discipline. Give up the urge to compete with others, or yourself, and focus on the joy of movement. Running becomes an obsession for some because they wish they could go farther or faster.

Giving up the urge to do more and replacing it with a commitment to getting more out of each session While seated meditation trains one to keep the mind focused on breathing, bringing straying thoughts back to each breath that is flowing out of the lungs is even more important when running. Through meditation it is possible to become keenly aware of the inward or outward world. Experience the movement of your body. Focus on the rhythmic striking of your feet on the ground. Experience nothing but each foot coming into contact with the earth. When thoughts enter the mind, acknowledge them, and then let them go. Bring your attention back to the earth. There can be painful, or at least, very uncomfortable aspects of distance running. Anyone who has attempted a marathon will attest to that. Scan your body and pay attention to how you are feeling.

Be completely present in the surroundings. Focus completely on the present moment and enjoy the journey.

On long runs, there can be adversity. Pain, fatigue, boredom can all become negative issues. Relax your muscles from your toes all the way up to your head. Bring the mind and body together in harmony. If your body is telling you to slow down or stop, you must listen. However, don't confuse a message that comes from the mind with one that comes from the body. Bringing your attention back to your breath or the rhythmic percussion of your feet hitting the earth can help you work through mental fatigue. During a period of strenuous physical exertion, the mind and body need to work in unison to overcome the discomfort caused by intense movement. Visualize the successful completion of your goal.

Running a very difficult trail in your mind can help you deal with the challenges you will face in life. Proper breathing is necessary to relax both the mind and the muscles.

Remove negative emotion from the experience. Be aware, but at the same time, detached. Know that your inner strength can overcome any external circumstances.

Don't worry about the miles ahead, only concern yourself with the moment you are in. Let the results go and just enjoy the experience. For an even more meditative experience, you can use a mantra while running. Attempt to experience all the senses of the trail.

When we run we experience a deeper scent of fresh cut grass in the spring, of the oils released by the plants after a rain, the hyacinth's aroma and pine cone smells from a wood burning stove, the ever so subtle smells of pies baking and steaks being grilled on the barbecues and the flowers, oh the glorious flowers in bloom and wonderful joy of those scents stay with us long after the run.

When we run we feel euphoric, running elicits a flood of endorphins in the brain we feel at peace as the meditative serenity takes us away. We also feel the environmental conditions, the incline in the road, the wind and temperature changes more intensely and the exhilaration of the power we possess. The view while running is at a faster pace, the Canada Geese overhead in formation moving above the runner but almost with him, the long line of pines acting as a border on the property the runner goes by, the sunrise in the morning is a magnificent view for the runner up at the crack of dawn and enjoying what most of the world never views.

Grief and the COVID-19 Pandemic

Grief comes in a myriad of forms and for vastly different reasons, but when the reason is a pandemic it takes on gigantic proportions of an international attack on humanity. Loss is the disappearance of something or someone that we value or valued in the past, present or future. However, in a global pandemic with more than a quarter of million dead it is a catastrophic event of unknown consequences. Each person listed as passing as I wrote this book created a grief process unknown to me in this lifetime. Loss is never simple, and it is almost always stressful and more complicated than it first appears to be.

The loss of thousands in a pandemic is tragic and complicated and can cause us to unravel based on when it happens and how long it takes to straighten things out. That reaction occurs on several levels: emotional, physical, behavioral, cognitive and spiritual. The grief process takes as long as the person experiencing it to get through, it can't be hurried, and it will stall.

My dear uncle taught me how to drive a car, the clutch, the brakes, the shifting, the alarming sound of metal grinding on metal from the standard transmission so prevalent in those days. Even though the grinding sound indicated a novice driver and stress on the transmission he never communicated impatience. He taught me how to grow tomatoes and lettuce and corn in our huge family garden. It was the most memorable and significant of my life. His patience and generosity which every good teacher uses to instill knowledge in their charge exemplifies a compassionate human.

He is now gone.

We must acknowledge the losses not necessarily accept it. Acceptance is much harder. We must feel the emotions including the pain. This is especially difficult when as a society we are used to doing and having many things at our disposal to lessen pain: alcohol, drugs and avoidance usually prolonging the grief. We have to establish new routines, do holidays differently, redo life in ways that work without the person. We must recognize that our loved ones live on through us.

We must recognize that all of humanity who perish in this pandemic were brothers and sisters and as the survivors continue in their image of light and love.

About the Author

Nora D'Ecclesis is an American bestselling non-fiction author and Haiku poet. Her bestseller *Spiritual Portals: A Historical Perspective* was #1 in the category of spirituality for over a year. Also in 2019, *Spiritual Portals: A Historical Perspective* won the New Apple Literary Award as the solo medalist in spirituality and International Book Award for best cover. Nora is a graduate of Kean University of New Jersey with post graduate degrees in administration and education. She has a long history of presenting events, retreats and seminars focused on wellness and stress reduction techniques.

Nora's published non-fiction include Amazon #1 bestseller *Haiku: Natures Meditation* and paperbacks/e-books on topics such as time management, guided visualizations, gratitude/equanimity, journaling and Zen meditation.

Recently, she added novelist to her list with the publication of *Twin Flame* written with her co-author, William R. Forstchen who is a New York Times #1 bestselling novelist. *Twin Flame* is a novella about a man meeting, courting and marrying his soulmate. Nora defines the holistic concept of twin flames in relationships. It is a blending of views about faith, love and perseverance from a universal spiritual perspective. The narration includes insights from Nora's expertise in Zen, Meditation and Reiki.

noradecclesis.com

Made in the USA
Middletown, DE
13 April 2021